THE BOOK OF PLANETS

AUTHOR: Clint Twist
ILLUSTRATOR: Kuo Kang Chen
ART EDITOR: Duncan Brown
EDITOR: Elise See Tai
ART DIRECTOR: Miranda Kennedy
EDITORIAL MANAGER: Ruth Hooper
PRODUCTION DIRECTOR: Clive Sparling

Created and produced by Andromeda Children's Books
An imprint of Pinwheel Ltd
Winchester House
259–269 Old Marylebone Road
London NW1 5XJ, UK
www.pinwheel.co.uk

ISBN-10: 1-86199-152-5
ISBN-13: 978-1-86199-152-2

9 8 7 6 5 4 3 2

Printed in Malaysia

THE BOOK OF PLANETS

CONTENTS

Mercury

Mercury is the closest planet to the Sun. It is a small, rocky planet marked by craters, with only the faintest trace of an atmosphere. Mercury can be seen from Earth with the unaided eye as a faint "star" in the night sky. Unlike real stars, planets do not always appear in the same place. They are called *planets* because they seem to move around the sky. *Planet* means *wanderer* in ancient Greek.

Myths and Legends

Mercury seems to move very quickly from one side of the Sun to the other, so the ancient Greeks and Romans regarded the planet as a messenger of the gods. *Mercury* was the messenger's Roman name, while the Greeks knew him as *Hermes*.

FACTS AND FIGURES

DIAMETER: 3,032 miles—about two fifths of the size of Earth

DISTANCE FROM THE SUN: 36 million miles

SURFACE TEMPERATURE: 333°F

LENGTH OF DAY ON MERCURY: 176 Earth days

SATURN

JUPITER

MARS

EARTH

Uranus is the seventh planet from the Sun. It is a gas giant and is only about one third of the size of Jupiter. The outer layer of the thick atmosphere has almost no visible features beside a pale green color. Uranus was the first planet to be discovered by telescope. The German astronomer William Herschel found this planet in 1781. It was so far from the Sun that at first he thought it was a comet. Only after studying the path of its orbit did he discover that Uranus was a planet.

MYTHS AND LEGENDS

According to an ancient Greek myth, Uranus was the god of the sky and the father of the Titans, who ruled the world before there were gods. Uranus was also the father of the monstrous, one-eyed Cyclops. Uranus was not the first-choice name for the new planet; Herschel wanted to call it *George's Star* in honor of King George III. Other astronomers insisted on a name from ancient mythology to match the other planets.

FACTS AND FIGURES

DIAMETER: 31,763 miles—about four times the size of Earth
DISTANCE FROM THE SUN: 1,785 million miles
SURFACE TEMPERATURE: -319°F
LENGTH OF DAY ON URANUS: 17.2 hours

Neptune is the eighth planet from the Sun. It is a gas giant about the same size as Uranus. The gases in the atmosphere give Neptune a blue color. Recently, spacecraft from Earth have photographed wisps of white clouds high in Neptune's atmosphere. Neptune was not discovered until the 19th century, following an intensive search of the sky. In the early 1840s, scientists studying Uranus became convinced that the planet's orbit was being affected by something else. The obvious answer was another planet. The likely position of the new planet was calculated mathematically. In 1846, German astronomer Johan Galle caught the first glimpse of Neptune through a telescope.

MYTHS AND LEGENDS

Neptune was the ancient Roman god of the sea. The ancient Greeks knew him as *Poseidon*. Neptune is often depicted driving a chariot pulled by sea horses. Neptune was also the god of earthquakes, whose anger was supposed to make the ground tremble. His symbol was the three-pronged trident traditionally used to catch fish. The trident is sometimes also used as a symbol for the planet Neptune.

FACTS AND FIGURES

DIAMETER: 30,775 miles—about four times the size of Earth
DISTANCE FROM THE SUN: 2,793 million miles
SURFACE TEMPERATURE: -328°F
LENGTH OF DAY ON NEPTUNE: 16.1 hours

DWARF PLANET

American astronomer Clyde Tombaugh discovered Pluto
in 1930 after months of studying photographs of the night
sky. When Tombaugh noticed a "star" that appeared to
change position, he thought he had discovered a new
planet. Some scientists refused to accept it as a true planet.
They noted that Pluto orbited at a different angle to
the Sun than the rest of the solar system, and that it
was more like a large comet. Despite these objections,
it was eventually agreed that Pluto was a planet.
In the 1990s, astronomers began to find other objects
that were very similar to Pluto, but even farther away
from the Sun. In 2006, astronomers downgraded Pluto
as a planet and re-designated it as a "dwarf" planet.

MYTHS AND LEGENDS

Pluto was the ancient   was to Hades by a
Greek god who ruled the   boatman named *Charon*.
underworld called   .   Charon was the name
the home of the dead.   given to Pluto's satellite.
The dead were ferried
across an underground

FACTS AND FIGURES

DIAMETER: 1,485 miles—about one fifth of the size of Earth
DISTANCE FROM THE SUN: 3,647 million miles
SURFACE TEMPERATURE: -375°F
LENGTH OF DAY ON PLUTO: 6.4 Earth days

Distance from the Sun (in AU)

MERCURY	VENUS	EARTH	MARS	JUPITER	SATURN
0.39	0.72	1.00	1.52	5.20	9.45

SUN

The Sun is a star—a gigantic ball of hot gas. At the center of the Sun is a nuclear furnace that produces vast amounts of heat and light. The surface of the Sun is about 10,800°F. The Sun formed at the same time as the planets—about 4.5 billion years ago.

MERCURY   VENUS   EARTH   MARS

JUPITER

INNER PLANETS

Mercury, Venus, Earth, and Mars are known as the *inner planets*. They all have the same structure—a hot metal core covered by layers of rock with a solid outer surface.

ASTEROID BELT

There are thousands of asteroids orbiting the Sun. Asteroids are chunks of rock that vary in diameter from 0.6 miles to 600 miles. Most asteroids orbit within the region called the *Asteroid Belt* between Mars and Jupiter.

Satellites

Most of the planets have their own natural satellites (moons) as opposed to artificial satellites sent into space from Earth. The most familiar natural satellite is Earth's own Moon.

MERCURY AND VENUS are the only two planets that do not have satellites.

MARS has two very small satellites, Deimos and Phobos, which orbit fairly close to the planet's surface.

JUPITER has more than 60 satellites. Four of these moons—Io, Europa, Ganymede, and Callisto—are more than 1,800 miles in diameter.

SATURN has more than 30 satellites. Five of these—Tethys, Dione, Rhea, Titan, and Iapetus—are larger than 600 miles across. The rest are much smaller in diameter.

URANUS has more than 20 satellites, four of which—Ariel, Umbriel, Titania, and Oberon—are larger than 600 miles in diameter.

NEPTUNE has 11 satellites. Of them, only Titan is larger than 600 miles in diameter.

PLUTO has a single satellite, called *Charon*, that is about 1,200 miles in diameter.

EARTH'S MOON

The Moon is Earth's only satellite. It is about 2,200 miles in diameter and orbits the planet at a distance of about 240,000 miles.

THE MOON

Io

PHOBOS

PHOBOS

Phobos is the largest of Mars' moons.
It is about 16 miles in diameter and
orbits the planet at a distance of about
5,800 miles.

IO

Io is the innermost of Jupiter's large
moons. It has a diameter of about
2,200 miles and orbits the planet at
a distance of about 260,000 miles.

Glossary

ASTEROID
A large chunk of rock that orbits the Sun.

ATMOSPHERE
A layer of gas surrounding a planet. Earth's atmosphere consists mainly of nitrogen and oxygen.

CANYON
A steep-sided, rocky valley. Most of the canyons on Earth were made by rivers.

COMET
A large "dirty snowball" made of ice, dust, and frozen gas that orbits the Sun.

CRATER
A roughly circular depression in a planet's surface, often surrounded by steep cliffs, caused by a high-speed impact.

GAS GIANT
A large planet with a thick atmosphere that merges into a liquid or possible frozen surface.

METEORITE
One of millions of small chunks of rock that travel through space.

ORBIT
To travel through space around a planet or star; the path through space made by an orbiting object.

PLANET
A large, spherical object that orbits a star.

RING SYSTEM
A thin, disc-shaped cloud of ice chunks that orbits gas-giant planets.

SOLAR SYSTEM
The Sun and all the objects orbiting it—the planets (and their moons), asteroids, comets, and meteorites.

SPACECRAFT
A machine designed to travel through space. Some spacecraft carry human beings, but most do not.

STAR
A huge, spinning ball of hot gas in space with a maximum size of more than 6 million miles in diameter.

SUN
The nearest star to Earth and the center of the solar system.

TELESCOPE
A device that gives a clearer view of something far away. Most telescopes use lenses and curved mirrors to magnify distant objects.

Index